To Do List Makeover

A Simple Guide to Getting Important Things Done

By S.J. Scott

http://www.HabitBooks.com

May 2014

Published by Archangel Ink
ISBN 149973445X
ISBN-13: 978-149973445X

Disclaimer

No part of this publication may be reproduced or transmitted in any form or by any means, mechanical or electronic, including photocopying or recording, or by any information storage and retrieval system, or transmitted by email without permission in writing from the publisher.

While all attempts have been made to verify the information provided in this publication, neither the author nor the publisher assumes any responsibility for errors, omissions, or contrary interpretations of the subject matter herein.

This book is for entertainment purposes only. The views expressed are those of the author alone, and should not be taken as expert instruction or commands. The reader is responsible for his or her own actions.

Adherence to all applicable laws and regulations, including international, federal, state, and local governing professional licensing, business practices, advertising, and all other aspects of doing business in the US, Canada, or any other jurisdiction is the sole responsibility of the purchaser or reader.

Neither the author nor the publisher assumes any responsibility or liability whatsoever on the behalf of the purchaser or reader of these materials.

Any perceived slight of any individual or organization is purely unintentional.

Your Free Gift

As a way of saying *thanks* for your purchase, I'm offering a free report that's exclusive to my book and blog readers.

Lifelong habit development *isn't* easy for most people. The trick is to identify what you'd like to fix and create a step-by-step strategy to make that change. The key is to know *where to start*.

In *77 Good Habits to Live a Better Life*, you'll discover a variety of routines that can help you in many different areas of your life. You will learn how to make lasting changes to your work, success, learning, health and sleep habits.

This lengthy PDF (over 12,000 words) reviews each habit and provides a simple action plan. You can download this free report at: http://www.developgoodhabits.com/FREE

Table of Contents

Why *Most* To-Do Lists Are Limited

Tell me if this sounds familiar: You start each workday with a lengthy list of tasks. There's a *lot* to do, but you're confident that every item can be completed. Then something unexpected comes up. Next thing you know, the day is almost over. You work hard at a frantic pace, but you end up feeling frustrated because there's not enough time to do everything.

Unfortunately, this is a common experience for many people. We all write lists with the hope that they will turn us into productivity machines. Sadly, to-do lists often have the opposite effect. The wrong *type* of list can be de-motivating, causing you to slack off and procrastinate.

The truth is anyone can write a list. The hard part is creating a list that's actionable and also fits into your busy life.

I feel part of our "to-do list problem" stems from a concept called the *hot-cold empathy gap*. Put simply, it's easy to forget about the action part when making a list. We all make those promises (like the classic "New Year's resolution") that simply can't be completed on a day-to-day basis. In other words, it's one thing to create a lengthy list, but it's a whole other thing to complete tasks when we're faced with dozens of distractions.

Another problem is that it's impossible to predict what will happen in the future. While you might start the day with a grand plan to complete an important project, you never know what crisis will arise from that next email or phone call.

When you think about it, the goal of a to-do list is to help you complete important tasks. So my question is: Why do so many people struggle with their time management and personal productivity? I feel the answer lies in how they create their lists and what commitments they make on a daily basis.

It's Time to Rethink Your To-Do List

There are countless ways to keep track of important tasks. From white boards on your refrigerator to the latest iPhone app, there is no shortage of options.

Unfortunately, the common methods of creating lists don't serve their main purpose, and most people fail to complete their important tasks and projects. More often than not, they fill their lists with a disorganized mess of tasks, wants, needs and random ideas. Then they sit around and wonder why they're not getting significant results in their lives.

The trick to getting results is to make your to-do list as efficient as possible. To do this, you must *rethink* the way you manage your daily life. Specifically, you should use multiple lists that cover different types of task. That's the core concept you'll learn in the following book: *To-Do List Makeover: A Simple Guide to Getting the Important Things Done.*

About *To-Do List Makeover*

The goal of this book is simple—I want to help you create lists that *actually* work. Like I said, *anyone* can make a list. The challenge is identifying the important tasks and knowing how to structure each day so you complete these items.

You'll find that the advice outlined here is fairly simplistic. I feel that's the real secret to being successful in life. Nobody wants a system that requires hours of daily effort. Instead, you'll find the following framework to be both flexible and easy to implement. My hope is that you will turn these lessons into an actionable, daily plan.

Who Am I?

My name is S.J. Scott. I run the blog
http://www.developgoodhabits.com/

The goal of my site is to show how *continuous* habit development can lead to a better life. Instead of lecturing you, I provide simple strategies that can be easily added to any busy life. It's been my experience that the best way to make a lasting change is to develop one quality habit at a time.

One area I'm constantly tweaking is my personal productivity. Like you, I've read countless guides on time management. And, probably like you, I found most of these books to be confusing, daunting and almost impossible to implement in a real-world setting. My time is precious, so it's impossible to spend an hour each day managing my productivity.

Like many people, I also used to keep one list filled with dozens—even hundreds—of tasks to complete. This was a blend of appointments, vague project ideas, routine tasks and looming deadlines. In other words, this list was a complete disaster.

The end result? I'd end most of my days feeling stressed and anxious because the important things were *not* being accomplished.

Eventually the stress got to me. One day I realized that if I wanted results in my business (and life), I had to fundamentally change the structure of my day. To start, I had to create lists that focused on results—not completing tasks for the sake of completing tasks.

What I ultimately came up with was a system that used **four types of lists**, each serving a unique purpose. And that's the core idea behind *To-Do List Makeover*.

It's not hard to create actionable to-do lists. All you need is a simple framework that fits into your busy life. In the following pages, I hope to provide you with an action plan that's easy to implement.

We have a lot of ground to cover, so let's dive into the content.

7 Common To-Do List Mistakes

(And How to Fix Them)

Most people don't put much thought into their to-do lists. Usually a to-do list is a mixed bag of urgent tasks, appointments and projects. The problem is that it's impossible to get things done if your actions are not completely clear.

It's easy to make mistakes like this with your lists, but the key to taking effective action on a daily basis is identifying these mistakes and finding a way to overcome them. Here are seven common mistakes many people make:

Mistake #1: Writing Lengthy Lists

Many people start their days with dozens of tasks to complete. Tasks often vary based on the amount of time they will take, the amount of preparation required and their order of importance. A list like this is often *de-motivating* because it's simply not possible to complete every item on a consistent basis.

The solution?

Write down no more than three "critical tasks" for each day on a small piece of paper. These are the actions that will have the biggest benefit, so they should be given top priority. It also helps to complete each task in order of importance. That way you're starting the day doing the one thing that will have the greatest impact on your life.

Reinforce the idea that these are important tasks by keeping this list in front of you at all times.

In addition, I recommend starting your day with one habit that drives your career (or business) forward. The idea here is that no matter what happens for the rest of the day, you've completed the *most important* task.

As an example, a year ago I determined that writing was a routine that's a critical part of my business. Now I always schedule a block of writing first thing in the morning before doing anything else.

Finally, people write lengthy lists because they have a fear of forgetting an important task. While I think it's important to map out the week, you shouldn't start the day with a massive list of tasks. Your never know what will come up and how your priorities will change, so it's better to focus on a handful of specific tasks.

Mistake #2: Being Ambiguous

Many people write down tasks without a clearly defined beginning or end point. You might think this acts as a helpful reminder to take action, but it usually causes stress because you don't know how to get started.

For instance, let's say you write, "Work on presentation." This is an ambiguous idea because it doesn't include specific, actionable tasks. You could phrase it better by writing "Watch five Ted Talks on YouTube," "Write a rough draft of my presentation" or "Think of three presentation ideas."

Remember, each task should include a specific action. That way, you'll know if it has or has not been completed. Furthermore, each task should also meet the following criteria:

- Includes a measurable outcome
- Can be done in a single time block
- Includes a clearly defined end point

We'll talk more about this in a later section of the book.

Mistake #3: Not Managing Your Time

It's hard to be productive if you don't know how long it takes to complete a task. We all have made the mistake of creating lists full of ambiguous items, but how often have you analyzed the time required to complete each task? Odds are it could take you anywhere from a few minutes to a few days.

Before starting any task, create a rough estimate of how much time you'll need. This gives you a simple framework of what can be accomplished on a given day. Even if you're wrong, at least you'll start to learn how to properly manage time. Obviously, this is a habit that takes some practice. However, if you do it on a regular basis, you'll get better at predicting what's *actually* possible to accomplish every day.

Mistake #4: Letting Random Events Derail You

Every day is different. We all experience emergencies and unexpected tasks that fall into our laps. While it's important to structure your day, it's equally important to be flexible.

Begin every day by checking your calendar. See what activities you have scheduled. Look a few days into the future to see what else you have planned. Then, once this is done, make sure you include *at least* an hour of free time every day for unplanned activities.

You'll find that creating a cushion for emergencies will reduce your stress levels. In your worst-case scenario, you'll have extra time to take care of random events. If nothing comes up, use this time to work on those not-so-important tasks that are cluttering your project lists (again, more on this later).

Mistake #5: Focusing on "Small Outcomes"

I know it's tempting to create lists that are full of seemingly urgent tasks. These are the items that might *look important*, but really aren't that valuable to your long-term plans.

Your daily lists should focus on items with true deadlines (like an important meeting) or an activity that has the biggest impact on your goals (like working on an upcoming presentation). The more you start your day with a focus on "bigger picture" tasks, the more you'll achieve.

Mistake #6: Not Connecting Tasks with Goals

Our motivation often comes from working on activities that truly matter. You'll find that when something relates to a goal that's personally important, you won't need willpower to get it done—it will be so important that you can't wait to work on it.

Before creating any to-do list, have a clear reason *why* each item is included. If you're writing down an item simply because it *sounds* like something you should do, then you might want to re-think its inclusion. The truth is that when a task is connected to a long-term goal, you'll feel more motivation and desire to get it done.

Mistake #7: Agonizing Over Incomplete Lists

As we'll discuss in the next section, maintaining four lists is the best way to stay productive. Some items are immediately urgent and others can be ignored if you have a limited amount of time. Regardless, it's important to remember that a to-do list isn't a life-or-death activity, so you shouldn't agonize over incomplete tasks.

Once again, my advice is to start the day focused on your three most important tasks. If you finish two of the three, then at least you've completed two important tasks for the day.

How to Overcome These Common Mistakes

It's not hard to fix these mistakes. While I've touched on a few basic solutions, it's better to see how each can be incorporated into an actionable plan. Specifically, the core philosophy behind this book is to stop relying on a single list and instead manage your life with four lists that serve different functions. So let's talk about how to do that.

Introducing Four Types of Lists

In the previous section, we talked about how some people take a scattershot approach with their lists. They add ideas, emergencies and looming deadlines to the same list, making it difficult to accomplish anything. When you think of how many folks use their email inboxes to manage tasks, it's easy to see how you might end up with a list that's full of both actionable and not-so-actionable tasks.

The reality is that tasks, projects and ideas are completely different from one another. Some are urgent, requiring immediate resolution. Others are ideas that should be acted upon—but *only* if you have free time. You can't start some tasks until you have a detailed action plan.

The challenge is that many people don't know what is part of a project and what is a separate, actionable task. In order to maximize productivity, you need to clearly define the activities that make up your days, weeks and months. The solution I discovered a few years back is to maintain four types of lists—each serving its own function. With this approach, you'll discover it's not hard to stay focused on important tasks and avoid the busywork that often masquerades as an urgent task.

What's included in each list?

Well, here's a breakdown of all four:

#1: Idea Capture List:

This is used as a dumping ground for every idea you'd like to pursue in the future. While some are immediately actionable, others will be ideas that never see the light of day. The key here is to develop the habit of adding to this list on a daily basis and reviewing it *at least* once a week.

#2: Project Lists:

If something requires more than two separate actions, then it belongs on a project list. This is basically a list of steps that take you from an idea to completed project.

#3: Weekly Task List:

We all have deadlines and scheduled appointments. They are usually a mixed bag of personal and professional obligations that need to be done on a certain day at a specific time. Before you schedule your week, it's important to look at this list and see what needs to be accomplished.

Project tasks should also go on this list. These items are the ones you need to complete to keep projects moving forward, so block out parts of your week to work on them.

#4: Most Important Things (MITs):

I alluded to this idea in the previous section. MITs are a small list (usually three items or fewer) of tasks that are your top priority for the day. The key is working on these items *before* doing anything else. With this strategy alone, you'll be far more productive than the people who spend the first hour of their day checking Facebook and responding to email.

Now, I know you might feel that maintaining four separate lists is needless busywork. Why should you do all this extra work in order to get things done? My answer is *clarification*. With four distinct lists, you'll have a place for every great idea, project task, deadline and daily activity. You'll also find it's easier to manage time when you start each day with a predefined roadmap. Finally, you won't suffer from a feeling of being overwhelmed. You get to focus on important tasks, and work on everything else *only* if you have extra time.

That's a brief introduction to the four lists we'll cover in this book. Now let's cover each in full detail.

List #1: Idea Capture List

Like I said previously, this list is where you deposit all the good ideas that you get throughout the day. You never know what will become a "million-dollar idea," so your job is to develop the habit of writing down <u>everything</u> that pops into your head—even if it might seem dumb at the time.

There are two primary ways to capture ideas: Evernote and the "43 Folders" system.

Let's go over each.

Method 1: Evernote

Evernote is a handy note-taking and organizational tool that can be used via the Web, on your desktop or as a mobile application.

This productivity tool uses a "freemium" model, which means the software is free with an optional upgrade available for more advanced features.

While the paid option is great for people with hardcore schedules or multiple projects, the free option is good for most people.

There are many advantages to using Evernote. This tool:

- Gives you a central spot for all your important work and personal documents, so you'll always know where your information is stored. That means you can keep personal content private in Personal Notebooks while easily capturing work-related content in Business Notebooks.

- Provides quick access to all of your knowledge in whatever form it takes. All of your notes, Web clips, files and images are available on every mobile device and computer you use—even when you're offline.

- Uses the Web Clipper feature, which allows you to create a scrapbook of links, files and images, all of which can be tagged and searched.

- Has a search tool, which will automatically search all your notes when you run a search in Google. This comes in handy when you have numerous links hidden deep in your notes.

- Syncs with scanning smartphone apps to take pictures of documents and then sends them directly to Evernote via email. Also, Evernote has OCR scanning capabilities, which means that *every word on the scanned document is identified and made searchable.*

• Can be used to organize important printed correspondence. Basically, your scanned documents can be filed, indexed and made searchable, which cuts down on the mountain of paper threatening to topple down on top of you.

• Works great with audio messaging. Simply record an idea and it'll arrive in your Evernote account. Plus, there's an integrated audio player that enables you to listen to your message without having to download it to your computer first.

Syncing Evernote from Mobile to Desktop

Yes, as with any good software program, you can easily sync all your content from your mobile device to your desktop.

Evernote is highly useful as a desktop note-taking application, but its real power lies in its ability to sync your notes to Evernote on the Web. This allows you to create and find your memories on virtually any computer, Web browser or mobile phone.

This means you can clip a *blueberry muffin recipe* from the Web on your Mac, read it on your iPhone or Android device when you're at the grocery store and then look it up from your friend's Windows PC when you're at her house preparing to bake the muffins.

Evernote is constantly updating all of your computers and devices with the latest versions of your notes, so you'll always have the correct information, wherever you are.

All of the Evernote applications are in regular contact with Evernote on the Web. Any time a new note is created or edited on any of your Evernote-capable devices, the note is uploaded to Evernote on the Web so all of your other devices will download it the next time they sync.

Method 2: 43 Folders

Ideas have a way of slipping through the cracks when you don't have a good organizational system. It's one thing to record a thought, but remembering to *take action* on it is something else entirely. Another way to capture ideas is to create a "43 Folders" system.

While David Allen talked at length about using an intelligent filing system, it was Merlin Mann who gave this technique the clever name of *43 Folders*. You can read an overview of the 43 Folders system in this post: http://www.43folders.com/2004/09/08/getting-started-with-getting-things-done

To summarize, 43 Folders is a systematic approach for following up on ideas. To start, you organize a filing cabinet with 12 main folders for each month. Next, you'll add 31 folders to represent the maximum number of days in every month. This gives you a total of 43 folders. The 31 folders are put in numerical order, right behind the folder for the current month, and followed by the folders for the 11 remaining months, as illustrated in the image below:

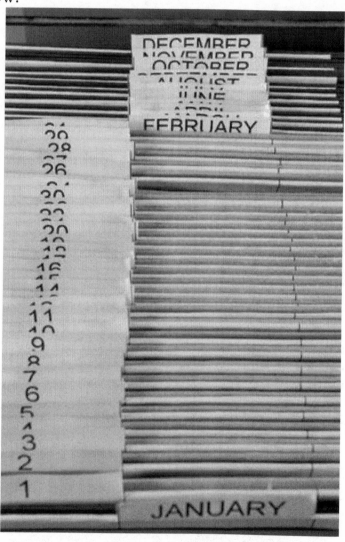

During a weekly review (more on this later) you'll create reminders to follow up on certain ideas on a specific date. Then the only thing you'll need to do is develop a habit of checking these 43 folders during your daily activities and taking action on any tasks.

43 Folders Habit Implementation

Developing the "43 Folders habit" requires a few expenditures, but it's a worthwhile investment to get on the path to never forgetting an important item.

Here's how to get started:

- 1. Dedicate a part of your home to processing paperwork and tasks.
- 2. Buy a simple filing cabinet and 50 folders with labels.
- 3. Put every task or idea into a centralized location.
- 4. Review these items as part of a weekly review.
- 5. Schedule a date to review potential projects or tasks.
- 6. Rinse and repeat.
- 7. Create a daily reminder to go through the current folder for that day.

43 Folders provides a simple mechanism for never forgetting an idea. When you create a reminder to follow up on tasks, your mind won't be occupied with random open loops. Instead, you'll be free to focus on current tasks and projects. Regardless of what program or method you decide to use, you always want to write down an idea and store it in a place that's reviewed on a regular basis.

Evernote vs. 43 Folders

As you can see, there are a lot of benefits to both the Evernote and 43 Folders systems. The question is, what is the best method for capturing ideas? In my opinion, Evernote is the best option.

Why Evernote? I like it because this platform syncs with every part of my life. For instance, if I get an idea while driving, I can use the voice-to-Evernote feature on my iPhone to instantly record it. Then, when I'm processing notes and email on my PC, I can use the Web Clipper feature to bookmark important websites. And finally, whenever I'm walking, I can record random, inspirational ideas. Pretty much everywhere I go, Evernote can be used to capture every important piece of information.

In *Getting Things Done*, David Allen urges readers to use what he calls a *ubiquitous capture device*. This is a fancy way of saying that all ideas should be kept in a single location. In my opinion, Evernote is the perfect solution for capturing all ideas.

List #2a: Project Lists

Most ideas involve multiple steps, and in many cases you can't complete them in a single day. That's why it's important to turn an idea into in an action-oriented project list. Here are some items to include in this list:

- A due date if there's a specific deadline involved—including milestones for specific tasks.
- Single actions and tasks. The smaller and more automatic a task is, the more doable it becomes.
- Separate projects for each idea. If you're working on five projects, then there should be five lists.

Seems pretty straightforward, right? Let's see how this would look with a simple work-related project.

Imagine today is July 1, 2014, and you're giving a keynote presentation on September 1, 2014. With a project list, you'd work your way backward from the presentation date, mapping out the steps you need to take along the way. You could break down the entire process into simple milestones to accomplish during the next two months. Here's how that would look:

1. Pick a dynamic topic to present at the conference. (Deadline: July 8, 2014)
2. Pitch the presentation to organizers and make sure they're happy with the topic. (Deadline: July 15, 2014)
3. Mind map an overview of what the presentation will cover. (Deadline: July 17, 2014)
4. Talk to the "target audience" and find out their current challenges/obstacles. (Deadline: July 22, 2014)
5. Collect relevant data, metrics and statistics. (Deadline: July 25, 2014)
6. Organize the information in a logical order. (Deadline: July 28, 2014)
7. Create a rough draft of the presentation. (Deadline: August 5, 2014)
8. Get feedback from colleagues; ask mastermind group members and friends for their input. (Deadline: August 12, 2014)
9. Write the second, third and final versions of the presentation. (August 19, 2014)

10. Practice the presentation until you're comfortable with the material. (Deadline: August 30, 2014)

11. Give the presentation. (Deadline: September 1, 2014)

Notice how this list contains a blend of single actions and habits? That means that not only do you need to complete each item, but you'll also need to set aside blocks of time each day to practice your presentation. This should be part of your *Most Important Things* list that we'll discuss two chapters from now.

Obviously, each project is different. The key point here is to start with the end in mind and then work your way backward until you figure out what needs to be completed.

One of the major problems people have with creating project lists is that they can't think of every task necessary to complete a project. While some people like creating linear lists (like a project list), others prefer the process of mind mapping. In the next section, we'll go over this concept.

List #2b: Mind Mapping for Project Lists

Mind mapping is a great way to create a detailed project list. Instead of writing it all down in a step-by-step format, you use a two-dimensional (often colorful) diagram that presents thoughts, ideas and plans in a non-linear fashion. This is called a **mind map**.

Here's an example of what this looks like:

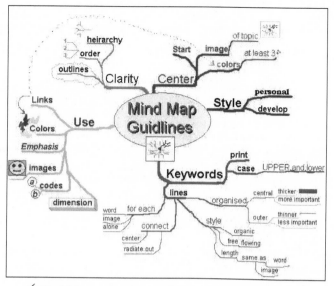

(Mind Map example provided courtesy of Wikimedia)

Mind maps engage both hemispheres of the brain. As a result, they are a powerful tool for planning, organizing and communicating a long-term goal.

With a mind map, you can also make an honest assessment of your skills, abilities and available resources. Anything you can do to come up with a working strategy can put you on the road to completing a project in a timely fashion.

It's not hard to hard to create a mind map.

Here is a simple seven-step process:

I: Schedule Mind-Mapping Time

Set aside 30 to 45 minutes for each major project. The time isn't set in stone because some projects require a minimal amount of planning, while others force you to think of many different variables. My rule of thumb is to dedicate at least half an hour for each project.

II: Ask Four Key Questions

Mind maps start with a deep understanding of each of your projects. Get started by asking these four questions:

- "What actions are required to reach the primary objective?"
- "What are my current strengths and resources?"
- "What obstacles will get in the way of my success?"
- "What additional skills do I need to develop to accomplish the main goal?"

Take a look at your past experiences with similar projects. Think of what you've learned from both your successes *and* failures. Then use this information as you create a mind map.

III: Start Mind Mapping

Go to your local office supply store and purchase a pad of drawing paper (or use the software I recommend below). I prefer drawing paper over normal paper because there is more room to write down everything you'll need to complete the project.

Once you have the right tool(s), you'll start mind mapping. Here are a few ways to map out your ideas:

- **Use keywords, lines, colors and images to express ideas**. A mind map is a visual expression of interconnected information that is easy to review and recall. Your brain processes information associatively, so connecting ideas in a non-linear fashion will help you determine the specific actions you need to complete.

- **Evolve your ideas naturally.** Start with a simple one-sentence idea. Put it in the center of the diagram and then surround the center with sub-centers that explain various mini-projects/ideas you want to complete.

- **Use a relevant keyword/image for each sub-center**. When using keywords, use lowercase letters, as they are easier to remember. The center is connected to the sub-centers by spokes. You can use different colors to highlight different themes and associations.

- **Draw arrows to elaborate on each idea.** From each sub-center, create an arrow that branches out. Use the arrow to explain what needs to be accomplished. You can add new ideas and actions as the project evolves. This is a free-flowing diagram, so you can delete/add items as you work toward completing the project.

IV: Identify Challenges

An important part of mind mapping is identifying the challenges that might hinder your success. There are three primary types of challenges:

1. **Outcome Obstacles:** Projects must be consistent with your long-term plans or what's *really* important to your job. If these are in conflict, then you probably won't succeed.

For instance, if you're pursuing a project simply to please someone else, then you won't have the internal motivation needed to take action on a daily basis. My advice is to avoid starting a project simply because it sounds like something you should do.

2. **Fears:** Fear of failure, self-doubt, lack of confidence and other fears can hold you back from taking consistent action.

Dedicate an area for your fears during the mind-mapping process. Take time to think about the "limiting beliefs" that might hold you back. Then come up with a few possible solutions. Odds are you'll discover it's not hard to overcome a fear once you've clearly identified why you feel a certain way.

3. **Roadblocks:** Sometimes external factors get in the way of completing a project. When facing external roadblocks, it's important to identify the actual problem. Simply review each potential

roadblock and think of how you'll respond if it comes up.

V: Avoid Censoring Yourself

Write down ideas as soon as they emerge without being judgmental or analytical. Sure, some might not seem that important, but they might lead to a secondary thought that has an amazing impact on your ability to complete the project. Allow yourself to follow through on every idea. Expand each one into branches and sub-branches and then go from there.

VI: Segment the Mind-Mapping Process

Our brains work best in five- to seven-minute bursts. During these bursts, capture as many ideas as you can and record those ideas rapidly using keywords, symbols, images and colors. Take a break for a few minutes and then go back to the diagram. Do this enough times to make sure you're fully elaborating on every possible idea.

VII: Turn Mind Maps into Action Plans

After brainstorming ideas, turn them into specific action lists. This goes back to the previous section. Simply think of what tasks need to be completed in chronological order, and then schedule them in your calendar for follow-up.

That's really all you need to do to create a mind map. It's a simple exercise that only takes 30 minutes to complete. Do it for all five goals to generate an avalanche of ideas with this multi-dimensional process.

Mind-Mapping Resources

Although I prefer the old pen-and-paper approach to mind mapping, many people like the technological approach to expanding on their ideas. Here are a few tools you can use for this process:

1. iMindMap (http://thinkbuzan.com/) is software developed by Tony Buzan, who many consider the inventor of mind mapping. It takes a slightly different approach to mind mapping than other software. While iMindMap is a premium product, but you can try it for free with a seven-day trial.

2. FreeMind (http://cnet.co/1fi0hlH) is a Java-based program with an extensive support wiki (http://bit.ly/1d4SNDR) that explains how to operate the application, create your own keyboard shortcuts and maximize your mind-mapping experience.

3. MindMeister (http://www.mindmeister.com/) is the simplest mind-mapping application. You can instantly create a basic mind map by using nodes, arrows and insert keys. It's fully customizable with node

colors and font sizes, and you can share your mind maps with other collaborators.

It doesn't matter what device you use to create a mind map. There are plenty of tools to expand on your ideas and map out the steps necessary to complete a project.

You have two basic choices with a project list: (1) Write down what needs to be done in a step-by-step numbered list, or (2) Use the non-linear format of a mind map to come up with creative ways to complete the project. No matter which one you choose, you'll eventually have to take action. That's what you'll do with the third list—the weekly tasks list. The goal here is to create a simple framework that allows you to manage time and focus on the tasks that will provide the biggest impact on your life. We'll look at this list in the next section.

List #3a: Weekly Task List

We all have tasks that require daily effort. These aren't part of a one-time project. Instead, they're activities that need to be completed on a regular basis. Examples include processing email, making phone calls and running errands. You also have to contend with random meetings, appointments and personal obligations. All of these items should go into a document called a **"weekly task list."**

Routine tasks make up the bulk of your day, so it's important to plan for them and add them to your calendar. However, it's important not to fall into the trap of blocking out every minute of your day. This habit will turn your weekly list into a grueling regimen that creates unnecessary stress.

My advice is to write down three types of items on a weekly task list: routine tasks that need reinforcement—like new habits; scheduled appointments, meetings and personal obligations; and important tasks pulled from your project lists. To illustrate this concept, let's go over each type of item.

#1. Routine Tasks

The weekly list isn't your typical to-do list. Instead, it's a collection of routine tasks you need to complete on a daily or semi-daily basis. These tasks are important for managing your personal and professional life, so it only makes sense to cross them off in a ritualistic fashion. I find that this list shapes the upcoming week.

Once a week, sit down and plan out the next seven days (I prefer to do this on Sundays). Start by blocking out time for these items: repetitive work tasks, exercise, errands, time with family, house chores, paperwork (both personal and professional), email, phone calls and cooking.

What goes on this list depends on you. The key here is to block out time each day for routine activities. It also helps to know how long each task typically takes. For instance, I know it takes me less than 60 minutes to process email every day, so I always leave enough time for this daily activity.

It also helps to "batch activities" together so you're maximizing each day. For instance, let's say every week you need to go to the grocery store, post office and hardware store. Then it makes sense to group these errands together into a single block of time. Doing these errands together will help you complete routine tasks in the most efficient manner.

Finally, there's a reason I recommend starting with routine tasks—it provides a framework for the upcoming week. If you're like most people, you're often bombarded with emergencies or random project requests. Without a set schedule, you won't know what will be sacrificed if you decide to say "yes" to a request for your time.

#2. Appointments and Meetings

In addition to routine tasks, you also have appointments, meetings and personal obligations. You need to account for these because your ability to complete important tasks hinges on how much time you commit to other activities. In my opinion, it's better to know ahead of time if your productivity will be limited because of previously scheduled appointments.

In addition to the weekly list, it's also important to maintain a digital calendar that sends a reminder when an appointment is coming up. This will act as a backup reminder for your important meetings.

There are a number of options when it comes to a digital calendar. Most mobile phones come with this feature, plus you can use Evernote or Office software (like Microsoft's *Outlook* program), which has a built-in calendar. My personal preference is Google Calendar (https://www.google.com/calendar) because it syncs with Gmail and is accessible via any device with an Internet connection.

#3. Project Tasks

The final items to include on a weekly list are specific tasks from your project lists. This process can be tricky because you want to focus on important tasks and avoid the temptation of overcommitting yourself over the next seven days.

My suggestion? Only include tasks that have a looming deadline or are considered absolutely critical to the completion of the project. Otherwise, feel free to keep an item on the project list and work on it *only* if you've completed everything else.

How to Create a Weekly List

We've already discussed three types of items to include on a weekly list. So how do you create a list like this? More importantly, what does it *look* like? The simplest way to explain this concept is to give you a sample action plan.

Get started by opening a Word document (or calendar) and dividing it into sections for each day of the week. If you're someone who works best at a certain time of the day (e.g., first thing in the morning), then sub-divide each day into AM and

PM activities. If you do a lot of activities on the weekend, then be sure to include Saturdays and Sundays. If you don't, then stick to a five-day schedule. This would leave you with a total of 10 or 14 blocks of time.

From there, schedule three types of activities: routine tasks, appointments and meetings, and project lists. *When* these are scheduled depends on your job and background. The important thing is to use this list to create a simple framework for the next seven days.

To illustrate this point, here is *my* weekly list that I'm following while I write this section (April 28 to May 4, 2014):

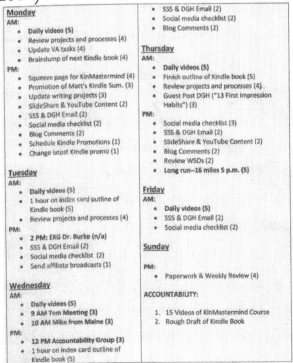

Monday
AM:
- Daily videos (5)
- Review projects and processes (4)
- Update VA tasks (4)
- Braindump of next Kindle book (4)

PM:
- Squeeze page for KinMastermind (4)
- Promotion of Matt's Kindle Sum. (3)
- Update writing projects (3)
- SlideShare & YouTube Content (2)
- SSS & DGH Email (2)
- Social media checklist (2)
- Blog Comments (2)
- Schedule Kindle Promotions (1)
- Change latest Kindle promo (1)

Tuesday
AM:
- Daily videos (5)
- 1 hour on index card outline of Kindle book (5)
- Review projects and processes (4)

PM:
- 2 PM: EKG Dr. Burke (n/a)
- SSS & DGH Email (2)
- Social media checklist (2)
- Send affiliate broadcasts (1)

Wednesday
AM:
- Daily videos (5)
- 9 AM Tom Meeting (3)
- 10 AM Mike from Maine (3)

PM:
- 12 PM Accountability Group (3)
- 1 hour on index card outline of Kindle book (5)

- SSS & DGH Email (2)
- Social media checklist (2)
- Blog Comments (2)

Thursday
AM:
- Daily videos (5)
- Finish outline of Kindle book (5)
- Review projects and processes (4)
- Guest Post DGH ("13 First Impression Habits") (3)

PM:
- Social media checklist (3)
- SSS & DGH Email (2)
- SlideShare & YouTube Content (2)
- Blog Comments (2)
- Review WSOs (2)
- Long run—16 miles 5 p.m. (5)

Friday
AM:
- Daily videos (5)
- SSS & DGH Email (2)
- Social media checklist (2)

Sunday

PM:
- Paperwork & Weekly Review (4)

ACCOUNTABILITY:

1. 15 Videos of KinMastermind Course
2. Rough Draft of Kindle Book

There are a lot of items on this list. Some will make sense in the context of the three types of items we've discussed, but others might be a little confusing if you don't fully understand the nature of my business. So allow me to go over a few points and explain why I've include certain items on this list:

Point 1: I'm currently creating a course where I teach the principles of being a successful Kindle publisher, which will be recorded in video format. To be honest, I'm not comfortable with verbally presenting information, so I reinforce this habit as a bolded task that needs to be completed first thing in the morning.

Point 2: I schedule *other* routine tasks, such as answering email, responding to blog comments and posting content on SlideShare, for the afternoon. This allows me the time I need to work on project-critical tasks during the first part of the day.

Point 3: I do my best to schedule phone calls and meetings on a single day—Wednesday. This is an example of how *I* batch tasks. By scheduling these tasks on the same day, I have more flexibility with other tasks during the rest of the week.

Point 4: I put personal appointments and their corresponding times in bold text. On Tuesday, I've blocked out an appointment with my cardiologist and time for an afternoon run.

Point 5: Certain tasks—such as writing and marketing—aren't included in this list. There are two reasons I do it this way:

1. Writing (for me) has become an ingrained habit, so I don't need the reinforcement to do it.

2. I start every day by focusing on three important tasks. Right now, the first task is to record those videos, and the other two are usually single actions pulled from my project list. Writing and marketing are usually part of these other two tasks, so they don't need to be scheduled separately.

Personally, I find it's best to not "clutter" a weekly list with a long list of tasks. I only include mandatory tasks and routine activities that require reinforcement. That way I don't feel overwhelmed by looking a list that's full of tasks I can't complete in seven short days.

Point 6: Next to each task is a small number ranging from 1 to 5. This represents the energy level that's required to complete that task, with (1) equaling very low energy and (5) equaling very high energy. Since I'm most efficient in the morning, I schedule the important tasks for the first part of the day. (We'll talk more about this in a later section.)

Point 7: Accountability will help you stay focused on the important things. Try joining an online or local group with people in your field to exchange ideas and get feedback. The reason I bring up accountability here is that you need to make commitments (to yourself and others) for what you'll accomplish before the next meeting.

Regarding my weekly list, I've made the commitment to complete 15 videos for the course I mentioned before, *and* finish a rough draft of my next book—the one you're currently reading.

Point 8: I take off Saturdays but schedule time on Sunday night to complete paperwork and process any new ideas. Then I'll print out a sheet I'll use to monitor my routine activities. This routine task list provides the framework for the *next* seven days.

Hopefully this example helped demonstrate what it's like to create a weekly list. Just remember one thing: This list should act as a *guideline* for what needs to be done. Life has a way of throwing curveballs at us, so it's best to view these tasks as helpful suggestions instead of mandatory items you *need* to complete. Honestly, life's too short to agonize over not completing a task or two.

Now there's one part of this process that we didn't cover in full detail—the weekly review. This is that scheduled routine for going over what you've accomplished in the previous week and making plans for the next one. Let's talk about *how* to run one of these sessions.

List 3b: How to Do a Weekly Review

The weekly review is a concept I originally learned from David Allen's book *Getting Things Done*. It's a simple process. Once a week, look at the next seven days and schedule the activities/projects you'd like to accomplish. Then process all the notes from list #1 (the idea capture list). You'll finish by processing any new paperwork.

You can accomplish all of this with three simple steps:

Step #1: Ask Three Questions

When starting a weekly review, ask three questions that will shape the focus of what you'll do over the next seven days:

Q1: What are my personal obligations?

Do you have a planned family activity? Are you going on a vacation? Do you have any personal appointments, meetings or phone calls? Is there something fun you'd like to do?

I've found that it's hard to complete projects when I have a lot of personal obligations, so it's better to *plan* for these potential interruptions rather than have them suddenly pop up and derail the next seven days. Honestly, you'd be better off reducing your output instead of trying to be a superhero by filling each day with 16 hours of activities.

Q2: What are my priority projects?

Sometimes a certain project takes precedence over everything else. This is the time when it's okay to *purposefully* procrastinate on other things. I'm a firm believer in focusing on one thing at a time. You can use the weekly review to focus your efforts on completing a single project that will have the biggest impact on your professional or personal life.

Q3: How much time do I have?

This question is extremely important. If you know your time is limited (like having a need to focus on a single project), then you should give yourself permission to not begin anything new. It's important to track the number of *actual* hours that you put into work and personal projects. Once you know, on average, how much time you spend doing different activities, can you use this third question to decide where to best allocate your time and energy.

Step #2: Schedule Project Tasks

After answering these three questions, map out the next seven days. The simplest way to do this is to look at your project lists and schedule time to follow up on the most important activities.

Take a close look at each project. Identify the items on these lists that will have the biggest impact on your professional and personal life. Then, schedule time in the next seven days to take action on these tasks. These are the tasks that will go on your weekly lists and most important things (MIT) lists.

Step #3: Process Captured Ideas

Okay, so you have a notebook/app filled with great ideas. How do you follow up on them? The simplest solution is to process each one and either do it immediately or schedule a time when you can act on it. This entire process can easily be squeezed into a weekly review.

Simply open Evernote (or 43 Folders), then go through each note. Basically you'll decide one of two things:

1. **The idea is actionable.**

   I'm a big fan of the classic "two-minute rule." The idea here is that if something takes two minutes to complete, then you should do it immediately. No putting it off and no scheduling time for a follow-up. *Just do it.*

If an idea is something you'd like to immediately implement, write out a step-by-step plan for how you'll do it. Jot down a series of actions you'll take on this idea and then schedule these actions into your week.

2. The idea is not actionable.

Sometimes you don't have time to take action on an idea, but you don't want to forget it. That's when you'll use the "43 Folders" system. Simply pick a date to follow up on the idea and then set a reminder for this date. That way, you'll never forget a potentially important idea.

Like I've said before, the weekly review provides a framework for the next seven days. By taking the time to process ideas, look at scheduled appointments and identify important tasks, you'll start the week with a focus on *what truly matters* in your life. And speaking of "important things," there is one list that will help you start each day by focusing on the big picture items. Let's talk about this concept.

List #4: Most Important Things (MITs)

This is where the action happens. Whereas the weekly list is full of routine activities and scheduled appointments, the Most Important Things (MITs) list focuses on three <u>very</u> specific tasks that will be accomplished on a given day. (Credit to Leo Babauta for this idea. <u>http://zenhabits.net/purpose-your-day-most-important-task</u>/)

MITs work best when you pick two tasks that are immediately important (like working on a presentation or a major project) and a third that's connected to an important habit (as an example, one of my MITs is always some type of writing.)

Another important aspect of this process is having a clear objective of the task with a rough time estimate of how long it takes to complete. That means setting specific, measurable objectives. For instance, let's say you're working on your next book. Instead of jotting down an MIT such as "Write next section of book," you'd want to set a milestone like this: "Write 1,500 words of the ____ fiction novel."

My suggestion is to set your daily priorities around the completion of these three items. In fact, try to do them (if you can) during the first part of the workday. That way, if an emergency pops up, it's not that big of deal because you've already completed the items that have the biggest impact on your life.

Finally, the trick to creating actionable MITs is to write them down either at the end of the workday *or* first thing in the morning. That way you'll have a clear understanding of the tasks that are truly important.

How to Create MITs

Creating an MIT list is easy to do—usually it's a habit that requires less than five minutes of your time. Simply follow these seven steps:

1. Use a Post-It note or small index card (this will prevent you from including too many tasks).
2. End each day by identifying three important tasks for the next day—or do this exercise first thing in the morning.

3. Prioritize this list, putting the most critical task at the top.

4. Identify mandatory routine tasks or appointments.

5. Wake up and immediately start working on task #1 until it's completed, then task #2 and then task #3.

6. Schedule any mandatory activities or appointments between the three tasks (how you complete these depends on your specific schedule).

7. Spend the rest of your day focused on other weekly list tasks.

I highly recommend developing the habit of identifying daily MITs. Starting each day with a focus on important tasks is a great way to complete high-leverage activities and avoid wasting your limited energy. You'll find that instead of "finding time" to get things done, you'll be working on priority tasks while most people are drinking their first cups of coffee and checking Facebook.

4 Types of To-Do Lists (a Quick Recap)

Again, you might think maintaining four to-do lists is needless busywork. However, when you put this concept into practice, you'll find it will help you stay laser-focused on each task. You won't feel stressed out, because things are getting done! And you won't feel overwhelmed by a laundry list of activities. Instead, you'll structure each day around completing the things that are truly important.

Before we move on to the next section, let's recap how each list is different and when you should use each one:

1. **Idea Capture List:** This is a tool (like Evernote or 43 Folders) that captures every idea or potential project. Nobody has time to do everything, so it's best to put all of your ideas in a central location that's reviewed on a regular basis.

2. **Project List:** If an idea has more than a few steps, then it needs to be fully developed into a project list. You'll find that taking the time to mind map the whole process will help you identify creative ways to flesh out what needs to be done.

3. **Weekly Task List:** You probably have routine activities and scheduled appointments. Before working on projects, it's important to identify these activities to make sure they're scheduled into your week. By putting them all in one place, you'll have a rough idea of how much time you can devote to the long-term projects.

4. **Most Important Things (MITs):** You can accomplish anything if you make a habit of working on important (i.e., long-term) tasks first thing in the morning. This is a simple habit where you write down three tasks on a sticky note and

use the list to focus on big-picture activities throughout the day.

These four lists provide the core structure of *To-Do List Makeover*. It's not hard to get things done when you put tasks in their appropriate locations and make sure they're being completed on a daily basis.

Here's our next question: *Where do I keep these lists?* More specifically, do you use the old-school approach by maintaining a physical list? Or do you go high-tech and use digital tools to manage these lists? That's what we'll talk about in the next section.

Physical To-Do Lists vs. Digital To-Do Lists

There are two schools of thought when it comes to managing to-do lists. First is the pen-and-paper (or printed list) approach, where you maintain physical lists that are kept in a binder. The second approach is to use software or an app you can access on different platforms.

Let's go over the benefits of each.

Option 1: Physical To-Do Lists

The first option is obvious—basically you maintain a physical list for all projects, your weekly list and every idea. You can store these lists in a file cabinet or a binder you carry with you at all times.

Many people like this option because you can refer to these lists when planning the week or working on a project. With a physical list, you don't have to pull out your phone or load a software program when you need to identify your next task. These lists can remain open at all times and provide structure to your working day.

For many baby boomers and members of Generation X, the paper list approach is more familiar. Here are a few reasons why this method works:

- Writing down tasks will actually help you remember them better than typing them into an app or program you don't regularly monitor.
- A simple piece of paper is often easier to find and use, given the large number of apps most of us have on our phones.
- There is a positive sense of accomplishment associated with physically crossing off items versus just deleting them off of your phone.
- You can maintain all your lists in a single binder that acts as an "operations manual" for your life.

That said, there are a few disadvantages to using a physical list:

- You don't have constant access to your lists. If you forget a folder, then you might not remember what tasks you need to complete.
- It's tedious (and not environmentally friendly) to print out a list every week.

- ** It's not convenient to bring a binder with you everywhere you go.

Now that you know the pros and cons of a physical to-do list, let's talk about the benefits of the digital versions.

Option 2: Digital To-Do Lists

Digital versions of to-do lists are great because they're portable, sync between multiple platforms (like your desktop computer and mobile phone) and provide a simple way to keep a historical record of your workload.

The key to finding the *right* tool for the job is using apps that have simple interfaces without too many bells and whistles. That's why I prefer a free app called "**Remember the Milk (RTM)** (http://www.rememberthemilk.com)." Here is a quick breakdown of what I like about RTM:

- **Manages tasks quickly and easily**. Offers an intuitive interface, which makes managing tasks fun. Extensive keyboard shortcuts make task management quicker than ever.

- **Syncs with** Android, BlackBerry 10, Evernote, Gmail, Google Calendar, iPad/iPhone, Microsoft Outlook and Twitter.

- **Get reminders anywhere.** Choose how you want to receive reminders. Options are email,

SMS and instant messenger services such as Google Talk and Skype.

- **Organize lists any way you want to**. Create as many lists as you want and store them in a cloud to easily see what needs to be completed.

- **Work together to get things done**. Share, send and publish tasks and lists with your contacts or the world. Remind your significant other to do his or her household chores.

- **Plan your time.** See what's due today and tomorrow, as well as the things you've missed. Prioritize, estimate your time and postpone with ease. This is great for creating simple MITs every morning.

- **Search your tasks the smart way.** Advanced search settings for finding things easily. Save your searches as Smart Lists, which are special lists created based on criteria defined by you. These lists are automatically updated as your tasks change.

- **Put tasks on your calendar**. You can manage RTM tasks alongside your emails and calendar because it syncs with Gmail and Google Calendar. This helps you review upcoming tasks, add/edit them and display projects—all while using your calendar.

- **Universally available.** RTM is on the iPhone, iPad and Android platforms. You can even use Siri on iOS to add tasks. It can even be synced with Evernote and Microsoft Outlook.

As you can see, there's a lot you can do with Remember The Milk. On the surface, it might look like a simple to-do list app, but you'll find it is a powerful tool you can use to manage the four types of lists that I recommend throughout this book.

Now, if for some reason you don't like RTM, here are a few other options you might want to consider:

- Any.do (http://any.do/)
- Toodledo (http://www.toodledo.com/)
- Wunderlist (http://www.wunderlist.com/)
- Minimalist To Do List (http://bit.ly/1nMKJgd)

Physical vs. Digital To-Do Lists: What's My Recommendation?

Okay, here's where the rubber meets the road. You have two choices: physical or digital to-do lists. What's the best option? Honestly, it all depends on your personal preference.

A digital version is perfect for people who are attached to their smartphones. Since they already manage their life through other apps, it's easy to develop a regular habit of creating to-do lists with a program like Remember the Milk.

Other people prefer the physical version of a to-do list—me included. What I personally like about maintaining hard copy checklists is that I can keep these lists open next to my computer throughout the workday. This acts as a reminder of what projects need to be completed and where I should focus my energy.

Ultimately *you* have to figure out what works best for you. While I have my own personal biases, at the end of the day, the tool you use should be the one that's the easiest to incorporate into your daily routine. My advice is to test both versions and see which one you prefer.

Creating a to-do list is just *half* of the process. Often what's more important is taking action on a consistent basis. In the next section, we'll talk about a simple eight-step process for achieving peak results with your daily tasks.

8 Steps For Achieving Peak Results With Your Tasks

Anyone can write down a plan for getting things done. The challenge is to actually *do* the tasks. Contrary to popular belief, your list doesn't really matter when it comes to completing important projects. What does matter is identifying the "right time" for tackling specific tasks.

The fact is your energy levels <u>will</u> fluctuate throughout the day. At certain times, you will be totally energized and motivated to tackle the high-level stuff. Other times you might be tired and unmotivated, only able to complete the monotonous and repetitive tasks. That's why it is important not only to plan your to-do list but also plan for the changes in your energy levels.

When you know how to best handle your energy levels, you can get more things crossed off your to-do list. In this section, you'll discover an eight-step plan for getting the most accomplished in the time you allot for daily tasks.

Step #1: Understand the Nature of Ego Depletion

"Ego depletion" is where it all starts. Basically this is a concept where people experience a diminished capacity to regulate their thoughts, feelings and actions as they work throughout the day. In other words, as you expend energy to complete tasks, there is less energy and willpower leftover. This will negatively impact your ability to complete other tasks.

You only have a finite amount of willpower. As you use it throughout the day, your willpower becomes depleted. This is why it's so important to tackle the difficult tasks when you have the most energy (i.e., at the beginning of the day or after a break).

Ego depletion happens to everyone and directly affects your to-do list. Realizing the impact of ego depletion and recognizing the best time to tackle important tasks are the keys to efficiency, productivity and crossing things off your list.

Step #2: Know When You Work Best

Have you ever heard of *circadian rhythm*? If not, here's a quick definition. A circadian rhythm is your daily cycle of activity based on a 24-hour time period. It is influenced by variations in the environment (e.g., the change from night into day) and affects your sleeping habits.

These rhythms affect humans and reflect how certain times of the day are better for completing certain activities. Peak hours of circadian rhythm for mental energy are 9 a.m. and 9 p.m. Peak hours for physical activity are around 7 a.m. and 7 p.m.

The tricky part is that there is no universal circadian rhythm. Put simply, some people work better in the morning and others love working well into the evening. Your goal is to understand when *you* work best and plan activities around your cycle of energy.

By planning your to-do list around these peak hours, you will have an effective approach to crossing tasks off your list. Let's say you're a morning person and want to consistently write 1,000 words a day. The best time to complete this task would be sometime between 6 a.m. and 9 a.m.

Step #3: Create an "Energy Rating" for Tasks (1 to 5)

After completing your weekly to-do list, there is one more step to add before starting on individual tasks: Rate each task on your list from 1 to 5. A task with a rating of 1 requires the lowest level of energy. Examples would be taking a vitamin or emptying your computer's recycling bin. A task with a rating of 5 requires the highest level of energy. Writing an in-depth article and exercising are examples of tasks that require your highest energy level. Use levels 2, 3 and 4 for tasks in between these two extremes.

Why is this important? If you don't know how much effort is needed for each task, then you won't be able to complete tasks in the most efficient manner. To start your day with tasks requiring the most energy, you have to know which tasks have the highest energy ratings. This will help you do a better job of planning your day.

Step #4: Start with "High-Energy" Tasks

The peak level of energy is usually at the start of each day. I recommend using this time to complete your MITs. You will be motivated, focused and have more willpower to complete any task you tackle because you're at a heightened level of energy.

Starting your morning off by completing a task and crossing it off your to-do list is also a boost for you to move on to the next task. You will experience a feeling of accomplishment, which is the perfect mindset for getting the important things done.

Trying to accomplish high-energy tasks later in the day is often a bad idea. Usually by the end of the day we're tired, stressed and distracted, all of which can lead to procrastination. Honestly, it's *really hard* to start a high-level task when you've already worked for many hours.

Step #5: Proactively Procrastinate on Low-Energy Tasks

On your to-do list, there are sure to be tasks that require less energy. These are tasks such as returning phone calls, responding to email and running errands. They don't require much focus because they're simple to complete. *These* are the tasks that you should save for the times when you're tired or unmotivated—like in the afternoon or after eating a large lunch.

For instance, checking and responding to emails is usually rated a 1 or 2 on the energy level scale. While this is an important part of most jobs, it should only be done after you've already finished larger, more complicated tasks.

Step #6: Practice Asking a Simple Question

We now know that (for most people) the beginning of the day is when you're at your peak level of energy, so it's important to start by working on your MITs. After that, you can go through your to-do list and look at the remaining tasks. The key when deciding what to do next is to focus on how you're feeling right at that moment.

Ask yourself:

"On a scale of 1 to 5, how much energy do I have right now?"

Maybe you say to yourself, "Eh, I'm at about a 3." Look through your list for tasks that have a (3) written next to them and start on one of those. This is a great way to match your energy levels to tasks you need to complete.

Step #7: Take Frequent Breaks

It's impossible to maintain a high level of energy throughout the entire day. That's why you need to take frequent breaks that allow for quick bursts of energy renewal. As mentioned before, your energy levels are at their peak after a break, so use breaks to your advantage.

The "Pomodoro Technique" is a popular method for time blocking and managing energy levels. The idea here is to completely focus on a task for 25 minutes, then take a five-minute break. You could do a number of things during this break: close your eyes for a few minutes, get up and walk around, stretch or have a quick conversation. The key here is to develop the habit of "shutting down" for a few minutes.

The 25 minutes on/5 minutes off pattern isn't written in stone. Ultimately, you want to figure out the amount of time that's best for you. Some people like to work for an hour before taking a 10-minute break. Others can do 90 minutes of tightly focused work followed by a 30-minute break.

My advice is to try a few different patterns before identifying one that works for you. Start a timer and try to focus on one task for as long as possible. When you notice your concentration slipping, stop the timer and take a break. Do this a few times, and you'll notice a pattern of how long can you can focus.

Step #8: Adjust for "Off Days"

We all have off days—they're a part of human nature. Honestly, there *will be* days when you're sick, tired, going through family issues or simply have a massive hangover. These off days will have a direct impact on your ability to get things done. That said, there is still a way to be efficient—even on those days when you're not feeling 100 percent.

I recommend looking through your weekly list and identifying those low energy level tasks—the ones with a rating of 1 or 2. Trying to do high-level tasks when you're not feeling it can be daunting and even de-motivating. Instead, save those tasks for a later day and do things that you can *actually* accomplish.

Sometimes you'll experience a lack of motivation that goes beyond an off day. Often you'll be plagued by an inability to get started on a specific task (or even *any* item on your to-do list.) In the next section, we'll talk about what to do when that happens.

How to Take Action (Even If You're Not Motivated)

Motivation is a very popular buzzword. It is seen in articles, posters and Internet memes. However, I feel motivation is often misunderstood by people. It's commonly thought that we work on tasks when we're motivated to and skip them when we're not.

The truth is motivation rarely has anything to do with our ability to complete a given task. For instance, I don't feel particularly motivated to write today, yet I still do it because writing has become an ingrained habit.

The *real reason* we often don't accomplish a specific task has to do with **fear**. That's right—deep down, we all know that starting a certain task or project requires us to overcome a challenge that scares us.

Don't believe that fear is limiting you? Consider these four beliefs that often hold people back:

Fear #1: Uncertainty

Sometimes you add a task to your to-do list without thinking it through. Then, when you work on it, you realize you didn't fully understand what needs to be done. This lack of understanding often creates anxiety because you don't know how to proceed. As a result, you keep putting it off because it's too challenging.

Fear #2: Failure

Sometimes even when you do your best, you fail. This feeling of failure sticks with us and can affect the other things we do. For example, if each week you're tasked with creating a report for your boss, but last week you didn't do it right, you'll probably feel a bit of hesitation before starting this task.

Fear #3: Difficulty

The more difficult a task is, the more you'll avoid it. This is especially true if it's a lengthy project that has multiple steps and numerous milestones. People often fear these tasks simply because they feel overwhelmed.

Fear #4: Frustration

Some tasks are frustrating, simply because you're not good at them. This causes you to ignore them or not take massive action. Unfortunately, it's not acceptable to procrastinate on projects in the working world. You have two choices: get better at the task or delegate it to someone who can do a better job. As you learned in childhood, ignoring something unpleasant won't make it go away.

Hopefully things are a little clearer after reading about these four fears. Odds are you feel some level of avoidance and procrastination when it comes to certain items on your to-do list. What's important is recognizing this fear and taking action in spite of it.

You might think to yourself: *"How do I take action against this fear—especially when I don't feel like it?"*

To take action, I recommend five specific strategies.

Strategy 1: Remove Distractions

After creating a to-do list, we all have the intention of completing every item, yet we often fail to follow through. Distractions are often the main reason why this happens. The trick is to get rid of the major distractions so you can take action on a consistent basis.

Here are some of the most common distractions and how to eliminate them from your day:

- **Email:** Receiving and responding to email throughout the day is the biggest killer of productivity. Instead of checking email constantly, set aside five minutes of each hour to respond to emails. Alternatively, make responding to emails a task that you do once a day.

- **Social Media:** You can lose hours of time each day to social media. Sadly, it's often time that's lost down a rabbit hole of Facebook status updates and Grumpy Cat photos. To avoid this, make sure you don't have social media sites open on your computer or phone while working. Honestly, it's best to have an all-or-nothing approach with this type of distraction.

- **Instant and/or Text Messages:** These types of messages can easily take you away from the task you're working on and turn into a 15-minute back-and-forth discussion. Put your phone on silent and out of sight, and close out of your instant messaging program.

- **Phone Calls:** Just because someone calls you doesn't mean you need to answer. Phone calls frequently turn into 20-minute conversations that leave you unmotivated and unfocused. Again, turn your phone on silent and set aside one time during the day to return your calls.

This brings up one of my personal favorite rules: *If it dings or rings*, turn it off and shut it down while focusing on a task with a high energy level rating.

- **Multitasking:** It's a common misconception that multitasking makes you more productive. In fact, multitasking can distract you from an important task and compromise the quality of your work. Make sure to stick to one task at a time and complete it before moving on to the next item.

- **Desk & Computer Clutter:** Both physical and digital clutter can distract you from the task at hand. Make sure your workspace is free of clutter to keep your eyes and mind on your work and off of a messy desk.

In addition, clutter can also compromise any work done on a computer. That's why you should keep your desktop free of random documents, folders and icons. Keep everything in folders that are clearly labeled and organized.

- **Noise and Chatter:** Office noises can be a major distraction if you work with a lot of people. A good solution is to wear noise-canceling headphones and listen to music that motivates you. The more you can drown out annoying background noise, the more focused you'll be on the important stuff.

Strategy 2: Write Down What's Stopping You

Just as it's important to identify your fears, it's equally important to understand the reasons behind a lack of motivation. We all have internal challenges that prevent us from taking action.

A quick remedy to this problem is to sit and write down the reasons you're not taking action. Do this for 15 to 30 minutes in a stream-of-consciousness or journaling fashion to get a lot of answers about what's holding you back.

Are you failing to complete tasks because you don't know how to do them? Are you attempting something that's beyond your comfort zone? Or are you required to work on a project that's not personally enjoyable?

There could be many reasons behind a lack of action. The key here is to learn everything you can about your underlying lack of motivation, which will be the ammunition you'll need to overcome it.

Strategy 3: Create a Plan for Each Obstacle

It's possible to overcome any obstacle that limits your ability to get things done. Here are a few common obstacles and how to overcome them with ease:

- **The task is really large or has too many parts:** Don't try to tackle a project all at once. Break it into pieces, turning the whole thing into smaller tasks that are easier to complete. Accomplishing the first task will boost your motivation to complete the next step, and the following steps after that.

That's why I'm a firm believer in creating project lists. The more you can break down a process into actionable steps, the easier it becomes to accomplish the big things in life.

- **You don't know how to do something:** If there's a task you're unsure about, get more information. Use every possible resource to find out more about what the task entails and how to do it.

You can search the Internet, ask someone who has done it before or find a book that teaches a task-related skill. Just remember that everything has been done by someone in the world. All you have to do is find the right person and learn from their experiences.

- **You are afraid of failure:** Fear of the unknown is a leading cause of anxiety when it comes to completing a to-do list. The best remedy for this is to simply take action. It's easier said than done, but we'll cover how to do this in the next strategy.

Instead of focusing on a potential failure, consider every obstacle to be a learning experience. Expect mistakes and challenges to occur. When they happen, take time to recognize what you *could have done* and how to handle it in the future.

Strategy 4: Commit to Getting Started

This strategy might seem overly simplistic, but getting started *really is* the best solution for overcoming a lack of motivation. You can't finish a task if you never even start it. The best lessons come from practice, not sitting around worrying about what you need to do.

One quick solution can be found with the concept of mini habits. A great book on this subject is *Mini Habits: Smaller Habits, Bigger Results* by Stephen Guise. Mini habits are small tasks that are brain-dead simple to complete. Your goal is to commit to the tiniest of tasks on a daily basis. Once you get started, it's likely you'll keep going.

Why do I recommend mini habits for getting started?

- **Success creates more success.** Mini habits prevent failure because they are small, quick and always achievable. The accomplishment you feel after completing a mini habit will propel you to complete the next task, and the next one after that, creating a wave of success.

- **Guilt-free.** Completing small habits makes the guilt of incompletion disappear. Every day you accomplish something will help you get rid of feelings of inadequacy or discouragement.

- **Strong self-efficacy.** Self-efficacy is the belief that you have the ability to impact outcomes. Completing mini habits trains you to always expect to succeed, which makes you feel more inspired to keep going.

- **More motivation.** Mini habits prompt action the same way a spark ignites a fire. The first small action begins the whole process. You start by completing a single repetition. When you start to feel motivated, you'll turn that one repetition into a solid block of work.

To illustrate this point, let me talk about how I recently used mini habits to overcome a major obstacle. In about a month, I'm launching a course that contains more than 70 videos. The problem? I absolutely <u>hate</u> public speaking and giving video presentations. The end result is I've procrastinated on this project for about two months.

Last week, Stephen recommended his mini habits concept during one of our conversations. Since then, I have committed to creating just one video each day. You know what's interesting? This technique really works. Usually after completing one video, I feel motivated to start another. Then another one after that. Usually by the end of the morning I've completed four to five videos—all because I used mini habits to get started.

Strategy 5: Understand the Rewards

This last strategy is one that has been proven to work for countless people. If you relate each task to a specific reward, you are more likely to complete it. Rewards create an excitement for working on a task. You can even create rewards for mundane tasks.

For example, completing a report correctly for two weeks in a row could result in a raise, commission or recognition from your boss. Always keep in mind how each task on a to-do list benefits you. It could be related to improved job performance, an increase in revenue or successfully accomplishing a personal goal. So when you feel like procrastinating on a task, think hard about what positive result will happen if you simply do it instead.

From "Low Motivation" to "High Action"

We just covered a number of strategies that can help you overcome a lack of motivation. But at the end of the day, everything is up to you. No inspirational quote or strategy will help if you're unwilling to get started. You need to commit to each item on a to-do list and focus on taking action.

In the next section, I'll show you how to do this. What we'll do is take everything you've learned up to this point and turn it into a system you can use for the rest of your life.

How to Create To-Do Lists That Get Results

The goal of a to-do list is to get things done. Oddly enough, many people spend more time planning things than they do taking action.

As General Patton once said, "A good plan violently executed now is better than a perfect plan executed next week."

It's important to heed this advice because it's easy to spend too much time planning out your day and not enough time *doing things*. That's why, in this section, we'll tie everything together into a simple action plan that focuses on helping you get results.

Action 1: Pick a To-Do List Platform

You have two basic choices when it comes to managing your to-do lists:

1. The paper approach with hard copies kept in a folder.
2. Digital to-do lists that sync between your desktop and mobile device (like the *Remember the Milk* app.)

The choice really is up to you. I prefer the paper approach because I like having a binder that's full of my projects and future tasks open wherever I'm working. On the other hand, you might like the syncing, multi-platform capability of a digital to-do list. Regardless of your choice, you need to fully commit to this platform and use it on a daily basis.

Action 2: Use Evernote to Capture Ideas

Evernote is one of the few productivity apps that I use on a regular basis. Odds are, you're constantly bombarded with ideas. The trick is to create a mechanism where you can follow up on a regular basis. With Evernote, you can record ideas and reminders throughout the day, then clip important articles while working on a computer. All can be stored in a central location for easy retrieval.

Action 3: Create Personal and Professional Project Lists

Any task that requires multiple steps should be put into a project list. This will be kept either in a physical folder or in your digital to-do list.

When creating a project list, use specific, actionable goals. Think of this action like you're trying to explain it to someone who has a limited understanding of your language. Be precise and describe exactly what needs to be done.

In addition, chunk everything down into short-term achievable goals. The more you can turn a project into a daily process, the more consistent action you'll take on it.

If you're having trouble figuring out all the steps in the process, use a creative tool such as a mind map to diagram every task. Keep asking "What's the next step?" and writing things down. Do this exercise for an hour to fully flesh out a project.

Finally, once you have a list of tasks, prioritize them in order of importance and immediacy. You'll use this information when scheduling weekly tasks.

Action 4: Do a Weekly Review

Set aside an hour every week to plan out the next seven days. I prefer Sundays because I'm relaxed from the weekend and energized to tackle the week ahead.

Focus on completing a few actions during this session:

- **Ask three questions.** *What are my personal obligations? What are my priority projects? How much time do I have?* Ultimately, the answers to these questions will determine what you should work on and what you should postpone.

• **Identify appointments and routine tasks.** It's better to know ahead of time if your week is full of appointments and meetings. That way you won't try to cram it full of too many activities. Doing so will only leave you feeling frustrated and unproductive. These prior commitments should be scheduled into your weekly to-do list before your project tasks.

• **Schedule project tasks.** Identify key projects for the next seven days. Then schedule in blocks of time where you can work on specific tasks. Put these into your weekly to-do list and treat them like priority appointments.

• **Identify required energy levels.** Write down a number—from 1 (low) to 5 (high)—next to each task on the weekly to-do list. This rating should match the energy level required to complete the task. Arrange the tasks so they match your personal circadian rhythms.

• **Process captured ideas.** Go through all your notes (from Evernote or the 43 Folders system). Create a short project list for what you'll do for each idea, or schedule a time to follow up on it. This is important because you'll never miss out on a potential opportunity.

That's it!

After completing this weekly review, you'll have a framework that will act as a rough action plan for the next seven days. Just remember to add some flexibility because you never know when an emergency will force you to switch up your schedule.

Action 5: Begin Each Day with MITs

Using your weekly to-do list as a guideline, identify the three tasks that will have the biggest impact on your life. Write them down on a Post-It note or small index card. Then start every day by completing these tasks *before* anything else. These should be clearly defined actions with specific starting and stopping points. More importantly, pick a metric that measures the successful completion of each task.

Also, plan to take breaks between tasks. Use this to time to relax, stretch, walk around or get a cup of coffee. This is important because it recharges your batteries before you focus on the next task.

Action 6: Just Do It!

This step is often the hardest for people. We all have those initial feelings of inertia before starting the workday. The solution? Simply focus on taking that first step and getting started. Here are a few ideas that can help:

- **Remove distractions.** These include dinging and ringing technology like email, social media, instant messages, text messages and phone calls. Distractions can also take the form of desktop clutter, background noise and multitasking. You want to start the day by focusing completely on the most important task.

- **Make preparations.** It's easy to put off tasks if we're not fully prepared to complete them. If you don't have the documents, email messages or software programs you need, you'll waste precious time looking for them. The key to overcoming this problem is to prepare everything ahead of time (like the day before) so you can immediately jump into the task.

- **Commit to getting started.** Stop thinking about how much work it takes to complete a particular task. Instead, focus on completing a really small goal or milestone. This uses the psychology of the *mini habits* concept I mentioned before—once you get started with a task, momentum usually kicks in and you'll keep going.

- **Focus on "The Now."** Stop agonizing over the many things that need to be completed by the end of the day. Don't worry about failure or what *might* happen. Simply concentrate on doing the best possible work you can in the time allotted for the task.

- **Create a plan for obstacles.** Take a few minutes to write down what's going through your mind whenever you get stuck. Is the task too complex to complete? Are you uncertain about how to do something? Do you have a fear of failure? The simplest way to overcome an obstacle is to identify the exact reason you're stuck and work on a plan to get past it.
- **Understand the rewards.** When all else fails, remind yourself of the long-term value of what completing this task means to you. The more you can tie actions to an important goal, the more motivated you'll feel to take consistent action.

Many people struggle with developing the "getting started habit." My suggestion? Start each day by removing every possible distraction, then focus on completing a series of important tasks to build positive momentum throughout the day.

Action 7: Complete Daily Activities and Appointments

Depending on your schedule, you'll also need to complete daily activities. My advice is to create a list of priorities. Start each day with your top MITs, then work on the items that are almost as important. Keep doing this until you end the day with the tasks that should be done but aren't life or death if they're not completed.

As an example, social media is important for my business, but I also leave it as an "end-of-the-day activity" because it's not as important as writing, creating content and responding to emails from customers.

Action 8: Fill in the Gaps

If you've completed the MITs and daily tasks, then pull out your projects list and work on the items that are next on the list. One of the benefits of maintaining project lists is that they provide a simple action plan for when you are unsure of what to do next. They don't overwhelm you because they are tucked away in a physical or digital folder, but you'll have them available if you have extra time to work on a project-related task.

Action 9: Make Hard Decisions

If an item stays on your list for more than three days, then it's important to do one of three things:
1. Start the next day by doing it immediately before you do anything else.
2. Schedule a date in your calendar to take action on it.
3. Delete it if it's no longer relevant.

One of the problems people have with their to-do lists is they constantly keep adding tasks without eliminating stale ideas. The end result is that they experience guilt because they haven't taken action on tasks that are months old.

Fortunately, there is a simple (but difficult) solution to this problem: Make hard decisions about each task on your list. If you keep putting something off, then you need to immediately take action on it or get rid of it. This shouldn't be a stressful activity. Figure out why you've put off some tasks on your list instead of ignoring them.

Step 9: Practice Continuous Improvement

No to-do list process is perfect from the start. Honestly, *I'm* still fine-tuning the way I approach my personal productivity. You may find that some of the information in this book isn't relevant to your life. My recommendation? Take what's personally useful and ditch the rest.

At the end the day, the to-do list system you end up using should match what you do on a daily basis. The key here is to test different time management strategies, learn from your experiences every day and keep tweaking the process.

Conclusion

(or "Getting Started Today")

Never underestimate the power of a to-do list. We live in a fast-paced, information-overloaded world, and sometimes it feels like we're being pulled in a million different directions. One of the reasons we're stressed out is because our minds are filled with incomplete thoughts and ideas. My suggestion is to stop *thinking* about them and start *creating* lists to guide your actions.

Moreover, to-do lists help evaluate the importance of a specific idea. If you find that you're continuously procrastinating or not taking action, then it's a sign that the task is not aligned with a personal goal. If you put an item on a list that's reviewed on a daily basis, you'll quickly figure out if it's really worth pursuing.

Lastly, I feel a to-do list allows you to clarify every thought that pops into your head. Getting great ideas is a commonplace experience, but it's a whole other ballgame to turn a random thought into an actionable plan, and then into a completed project. With a to-do list, you can map out every step of a process and turn it into a daily action plan.

Our time together is at an end. You now know why it's important to create four types of lists and you've learned a simple blueprint for getting started. The rest is up to you.

It's okay if you make mistakes along the way. That's how we all learn those important lessons in life.

Your top priority is to stay committed to the process. Each week—in fact, *each day*—you're given an opportunity to create lists that help you get things done. All you have to do is learn from this daily experience and apply the lessons you learn along the way.

I wish you the best of luck.

S.J. Scott
Author: http://www.HabitBooks.com
Blog: http://www.DevelopGoodHabits.com

Would You Like to Know More?

Often it's easy to procrastinate on developing new habits. You ignore them because you're paralyzed by uncertainty and what's required to make things happen in your life.

One way to fix this problem is to adopt an "anti-procrastination" mindset. When you know *how* to take action on a consistent basis, you can accomplish anything. In my book, *23 Anti-Procrastination Habits*, you'll get a series of simple-to-follow routines that can help not only build new habits, but can increase your productivity in many different areas.

You can learn more here:
http://www.developgoodhabits.com/book-23aph

Thank You

Before you go, I'd like to say "thank you" for purchasing my guide.

I know you could have picked from dozens of books on habit development, but you took a chance with my system.

So a big thanks for ordering this book and reading all the way to the end.

Now I'd like ask for a *small* favor. Could you please take a minute or two and leave a review for this book on Amazon?

http://www.developgoodhabits.com/todo-book

This feedback will help me continue to write the kind of books that help you get results. And if you loved it, then please let me know :-)

More Books by S.J. Scott

- *23 Anti-Procrastination Habits: How to Stop Being Lazy and Get Results In Your Life*

- *S.M.A.R.T. Goals Made Simple: 10 Steps to Master Your Personal and Career Goals*

- *Writing Habit Mastery: How to Write 2,000 Words a Day and Forever Cure Writer's Block*

- *Declutter Your Inbox: 9 Proven Steps to Eliminate Email Overload*

- *Wake Up Successful: How to Increase Your Energy and Achieve Any Goal with a Morning Routine*

- *10,000 Steps Blueprint: The Daily Walking Habit for Healthy Weight Loss and Lifelong Fitness*

- *70 Healthy Habits: How to Eat Better, Feel Great, Get More Energy and Live a Healthy Lifestyle*

- *Resolutions That Stick! How 12 Habits Can Transform Your New Year*

About the Author

"Build a Better Life - One Habit at a Time"

Getting more from life doesn't mean following the latest diet craze or motivation program. True success happens when you take action on a daily basis. In other words, it's your habits that help you achieve goals and live the life you've always wanted.

In his books, S.J. provides daily action plans for every area of your life: health, fitness, work and personal relationships. Unlike other personal development guides, his content focuses on taking action. So instead of reading over-hyped strategies that rarely work in the real-world, you'll get information that can be immediately implemented

When not writing, S.J. likes to read, exercise and explore the different parts of the world.

Made in the USA
Lexington, KY
02 February 2017